BIOGRAPHY

Introducing Mohamed Abdell, an Egyptian and Australian executive chef with over 25 years of experience working in some of the world's top luxury hotels. With a Bachelor's degree in Hotel Management and expertise in multiple cuisines, Mohamed is a culinary mastermind. He has worked in renowned hotels such as Four Seasons, Intercontinental, Sheraton, Crystalbrook, and Marriott Hotel. His experience spans across the globe, from Egypt, Singapore, and Macau to Australia.

Mohamed's diverse cultural heritage and exposure to various cuisines have influenced his approach to cooking, resulting in an innovative and eclectic style. His expertise in Middle Eastern cuisine, Italian cuisine, Mediterranean cuisine, French, modern cuisine, Australian cuisine, and an awareness of Asian cuisine such as Thailand and Japanese, make him a standout chef in the industry.

Mohamed's passion for food and commitment to excellence is evident in every dish he creates. He continually pushes the boundaries of traditional cooking, always seeking to innovate and experiment with new techniques and flavors. His extensive experience and multicultural background make him a dynamic and inspiring figure in the culinary world.

BOOK INTRODUCTION

Drying fish is a technique that has been used for centuries to preserve this valuable source of protein. In many parts of the world, drying fish is still a common practice, and it is an important part of the local cuisine. However, despite its importance, the art of drying fish is not well understood by many people.

In this comprehensive guide, we will explore the various techniques and methods used for drying fish. From the history of drying fish to the tools and equipment needed, to the different types of fish suitable for drying, this book covers everything you need to know about this age-old preservation method.

Whether you are a professional fisherman or someone who wants to learn more about preserving food, this book is for you. We will cover outdoor and indoor drying techniques, smoking fish for preservation, and even how to store and package dried fish.

But the art of drying fish is not just about preserving food. It also has cultural significance in many parts of the world. We will explore the cultural significance of drying fish and how it is an important part of the local cuisine in many countries.

So, whether you are looking to preserve your catch or simply want to learn more about this fascinating technique, this book is the ultimate guide to the art of drying fish.

TABLE OF CONTENT

CHAPTER 1:
The History of Drying Fish

Drying fish is a preservation method that has been used for thousands of years. In many parts of the world, it is still a common practice, and it is an important part of the local cuisine. But where did this technique originate, and how has it evolved over time?

The history of drying fish dates back to ancient times. The Egyptians, Greeks, and Romans all practiced some form of fish preservation, including drying fish. In Europe, dried fish was a staple food during the Middle Ages, and it was an important trade item in the Nordic countries.

In North America, the indigenous peoples used drying fish as a way to preserve their catch for the winter months. The Inuit people, for example, would dry fish on wooden racks outside their homes. The dried fish would then be stored for the winter months when fresh food was scarce. As the world became more connected through trade and exploration, dried fish became an important commodity. European explorers brought dried fish with them on long sea voyages, and it became a popular food item in many countries.

Today, drying fish is still a common practice in many parts of the world, including Scandinavia, Africa, and Asia. In some countries, it is an important part of the local cuisine, and dried fish is used in a variety of dishes.

As we continue to explore the art of drying fish, it is important to understand its rich history and cultural significance. By understanding the origins of this preservation method, we can appreciate its importance and continue to improve upon the techniques used to this day.

CHAPTER 2:
Types of Fish Suitable for Dry Aging

Not all types of fish are suitable for drying, and some species are better suited for this preservation method than others. In this chapter, we will explore the types of fish that are most commonly used for drying and why they are well-suited for this technique.

1. **Cod:** Cod is one of the most popular fish for drying. Its firm texture and mild flavor make it ideal for this preservation method. Cod is commonly used for making stockfish, a type of dried fish that is a staple in many Scandinavian countries.

2. **Haddock:** Haddock is another white fish that is commonly used for drying. It has a slightly sweeter flavor than cod and is often used to make smoked haddock, a popular ingredient in Scottish cuisine.

3. **Mackerel:** Mackerel is a fatty fish that is well-suited for smoking and drying. Its rich flavor and oily texture make it a popular choice for making smoked and dried fish products.

4. **Salmon:** Salmon is a popular fish for smoking, but it is also well-suited for drying. Its firm texture and rich flavor make it a great choice for making salmon jerky or smoked salmon.

5. **Tuna:** Tuna is a meaty fish that is commonly used for making jerky. Its dense flesh and mild flavor make it a great choice for this preservation method.

6. **Sardines:** Sardines are a small, oily fish that are often used for canning or smoking. They are also well-suited for drying, and their small size makes them a convenient snack for on-the-go.

When selecting fish for drying, it is important to choose fish that are fresh and have not been previously frozen. Fresh fish will have a better texture and flavor when dried. Additionally, it is important to choose fish that are high in fat content, as this will help to preserve the fish and give it a rich flavor.

In conclusion, there are several types of fish that are well-suited for drying, including cod, haddock, mackerel, salmon, tuna, and sardines. These fish are chosen for their texture, flavor, and fat content, which make them ideal for this preservation method. When selecting fish for drying, it is important to choose fresh fish that have not been previously frozen to ensure the best results.

CHAPTER 3:
Tools and Equipment for Drying Aged Fish

Properly drying aged fish requires the use of specific tools and equipment. In this chapter, we will explore the tools and equipment necessary for drying aged fish.

1. **Drying Racks:** Drying racks are essential for drying aged fish. They come in various sizes and shapes, but all have a flat surface on which to lay the fish. The racks should be made of a material that is easy to clean and can withstand exposure to salt and moisture.

2. **Salt:** Salt is a crucial ingredient in the drying process. It helps to preserve the fish and also adds flavor. Sea salt is the preferred type of salt for drying fish.

3. **Knife:** A sharp knife is necessary for preparing the fish for drying. It should be able to cleanly cut through the fish and remove any bones or skin.

4. **Fish Scaler:** A fish scaler is used to remove the scales from the fish before it is dried. This tool helps to make the drying process more efficient and ensures that all of the scales are removed.

5. **Smoking Chips:** Smoking chips are used to add flavor to the fish during the drying process. They come in a variety of flavors, such as hickory, mesquite, and applewood.

6. **Dehydrator:** A dehydrator is an electric device that can be used to dry aged fish. It works by circulating warm air over the fish, removing moisture and preserving the fish.

7. **Humidity Monitor:** A humidity monitor is used to monitor the humidity levels during the drying process. This is important because the ideal humidity level will vary depending on the type of fish being dried.

8. **Vacuum Sealer:** A vacuum sealer is used to store the dried aged fish. It removes all of the air from the packaging, which helps to preserve the fish and extend its shelf life.

In conclusion, the tools and equipment necessary for drying aged fish include drying racks, salt, a knife, fish scaler, smoking chips, a dehydrator, a humidity monitor, and a vacuum sealer. Each of these tools plays an important role in the drying process and ensures that the fish is properly prepared, preserved, and stored. When selecting tools and equipment for drying aged fish, it is important to choose high-quality items that are durable and easy to use.

CHAPTER 4:
Preparing the Fish for Drying

Before you can begin the process of drying aged fish, it is important to properly prepare the fish. In this chapter, we will discuss the steps involved in preparing the fish for drying.

1. **Cleaning:** The first step in preparing the fish for drying is cleaning. Rinse the fish under cold water to remove any dirt or debris. If the fish still has scales, use a fish scaler to remove them. Once the fish is clean and scaled, remove the head, tail, and guts.

2. **Filleting:** Use a sharp knife to fillet the fish. Start by making a cut along the spine, and then use a gentle sawing motion to remove the fillet. Cut away any remaining bones or skin, and then rinse the fillet under cold water.

3. **Salting:** Salt is a crucial ingredient in the drying process. Rub a generous amount of salt onto the flesh of the fillet, making sure to cover both sides evenly. Allow the salt to sit on the fillet for at least 30 minutes, or up to a few hours, depending on the size of the fillet.

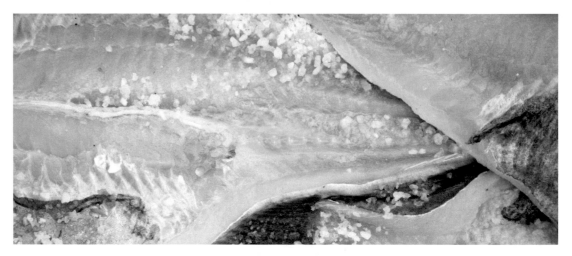

4. **Drying:** After salting, rinse the fillet under cold water to remove excess salt. Pat the fillet dry with a clean towel or paper towel, and then place it on a drying rack. Allow the fillet to air dry for several hours, or until the flesh has a firm texture and the surface of the fish is dry.

5. **Smoking:** Smoking is an optional step in the drying process, but it can add a rich flavor to the fish. To smoke the fish, soak smoking chips in water for at least 30 minutes, and then place them in a smoker. Place the drying racks with the fish onto the smoker rack, and then smoke the fish for several hours, or until the desired level of smokiness is achieved.

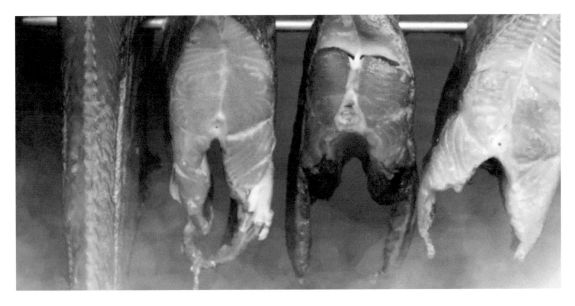

6. **Storing:** Once the fish has been dried and smoked (if desired), it can be stored. Vacuum seal the fish in a plastic bag, and then store it in the refrigerator for up to several weeks, or in the freezer for up to several months.

In conclusion, preparing the fish for drying requires cleaning, filleting, salting, drying, smoking (if desired), and storing. Each step is crucial to the overall quality and taste of the dried aged fish. It is important to use high-quality fish, salt, and smoking chips, and to ensure that the fish is properly cleaned and dried before smoking and storing. With these steps in mind, you can successfully prepare fish for drying and enjoy the delicious results.

CHAPTER 5:
Choosing the Right Drying Method

There are several methods for drying aged fish, each with its own advantages and disadvantages. In this chapter, we will discuss the different methods for drying aged fish and how to choose the right method for your needs.

1. **Sun Drying:** Sun drying is one of the oldest and most traditional methods for drying fish. This method involves placing the fish on drying racks in the sun and allowing the sun to dry the fish naturally. The advantages of sun drying are that it is simple, low-cost, and requires no special equipment. However, the disadvantages are that it can be affected by the weather, takes longer than other methods, and may result in lower quality fish if not done properly.

2. **Oven Drying:** Oven drying involves placing the fish on drying racks and drying it in an oven at a low temperature. The advantages of oven drying are that it is faster than sun and air drying, and the temperature and humidity can be controlled more easily. However, the disadvantages are that it requires a special oven with a low-temperature setting and can be more expensive than other methods.

3. **Dehydrator Drying:** Dehydrator drying involves using a dehydrator to dry the fish. The advantages of dehydrator drying are that it is faster than sun and air drying, and the temperature and humidity can be controlled more easily. However, the disadvantages are that it requires a special dehydrator and can be more expensive than other methods.

When choosing the right drying method for your needs, consider the advantages and disadvantages of each method, as well as the cost, time, and equipment required. Factors such as the climate in your area, the amount of fish you need to dry, and your budget will also play a role in your decision.

In conclusion, there are several methods for drying aged fish, each with its own advantages and disadvantages. When choosing the right method, consider factors such as cost, time, equipment required, and the climate in your area. With the right method, you can successfully dry aged fish and enjoy the delicious results.

CHAPTER 6:
Outdoor Drying Techniques

Outdoor drying is one of the oldest and most traditional methods for drying fish. This method involves placing the fish on drying racks in an outdoor area and allowing the sun and air to dry the fish naturally. In this chapter, we will discuss the different outdoor drying techniques for drying aged fish.

1. **Sun Drying:** Sun drying is the most common outdoor drying technique. It involves placing the fish on drying racks in an outdoor area that receives direct sunlight. The sun's heat and UV rays help to dry the fish naturally, while the wind helps to circulate air around the fish. The advantages of sun drying are that it is low-cost, requires no special equipment, and results in a unique flavor and texture. However, the disadvantages are that it can be affected by the weather and may result in lower quality fish if not done properly.

2. **Smoke Drying:** Smoke drying is another outdoor drying technique that has been used for centuries. This method involves smoking the fish over a fire or smoker. The smoke not only helps to dry the fish but also adds a delicious smoky flavor. The advantages of smoke drying are that it results in a unique flavor and texture and helps to preserve the fish for a longer period. However, the disadvantages are that it requires special equipment and can be time-consuming.

3. **Wind Drying:** Wind drying involves placing the fish on drying racks in an outdoor area that receives a steady breeze. The wind helps to circulate air around the fish and dry it naturally. The advantages of wind drying are that it is low-cost, requires no special equipment, and results in a unique flavor and texture. However, the disadvantages are that it can be affected by the weather and may take longer than other methods.

4. **Salt Drying:** Salt drying is a technique that has been used for centuries to preserve fish. This method involves salting the fish and leaving it to dry in an outdoor area. The salt helps to draw out moisture from the fish and preserve it for a longer period. The advantages of salt drying are that it helps to preserve the fish for a longer period and results in a unique flavor and texture. However, the disadvantages are that it requires a large amount of salt and can be time-consuming.

When choosing an outdoor drying technique, consider factors such as the weather in your area, the amount of fish you need to dry, and the flavor and texture you want to achieve. With the right technique, you can successfully dry aged fish outdoors and enjoy the delicious results.

CHAPTER 7:
Indoor Drying Techniques

While outdoor drying is a popular and traditional method for drying aged fish, indoor drying techniques can also be effective. In this chapter, we will discuss the different indoor drying techniques for drying aged fish.

1. **Air Drying:** Air drying is the most common indoor drying technique. It involves placing the fish on drying racks in a well-ventilated indoor area. The air helps to dry the fish naturally, while the racks help to promote airflow around the fish. The advantages of air drying are that it can be done indoors, regardless of the weather, and results in a unique flavor and texture. However, the disadvantages are that it can take longer than other methods and may require special equipment for proper ventilation.

2. **Dehydrator Drying:** Dehydrator drying is a method that involves using an electric dehydrator to dry the fish. The dehydrator has a series of trays that hold the fish and uses a fan to circulate warm air around them. The advantages of dehydrator drying are that it is a quick and efficient method, requires minimal monitoring, and results in consistent quality fish. However, the disadvantages are that it requires a special dehydrator and may result in a less unique flavor and texture.

3. **Oven Drying:** Oven drying is a method that involves using an oven to dry the fish. The fish is placed on a baking sheet and baked at a low temperature for several hours. The advantages of oven drying are that it is a quick and efficient method and requires minimal monitoring. However, the disadvantages are that it can result in a less unique flavor and texture and may require special equipment for proper ventilation.

4. **Freeze Drying:** Freeze drying is a method that involves freezing the fish and then removing the moisture by placing it in a vacuum chamber. This method is more commonly used for preserving food, but it can also be used for drying aged fish. The advantages of freeze drying are that it preserves the nutritional value of the fish and results in a consistent quality product. However, the disadvantages are that it requires special equipment and can be expensive.

When choosing an indoor drying technique, consider factors such as the amount of fish you need to dry, the space available, and the flavor and texture you want to achieve. With the right technique, you can successfully dry aged fish indoors and enjoy the delicious results.

CHAPTER 8:
Sun Drying vs. Oven Drying

When it comes to drying aged fish, there are several methods to choose from, including sun drying and oven drying. In this chapter, we will compare and contrast the two methods to help you decide which one is right for you.

Sun Drying

Sun drying is a traditional method for drying fish that has been used for centuries. It involves placing the fish on drying racks in the sun and allowing them to dry naturally. The advantages of sun drying are that it is a natural method that does not require any special equipment, and it produces a unique flavor and texture. However, the disadvantages are that it can be time-consuming and requires a lot of space for the racks.

Oven Drying

Oven drying is a more modern method that involves using an oven to dry the fish. The fish is placed on a baking sheet and baked at a low temperature for several hours. The advantages of oven drying are that it is a quick and efficient method that requires minimal space and produces a consistent quality product. However, the disadvantages are that it requires special equipment and can result in a less unique flavor and texture.

Comparison

When comparing sun drying and oven drying, there are several factors to consider. These include:

1. **Time:** Sun drying can take longer than oven drying, as it relies on the sun and weather conditions. Oven drying, on the other hand, is a quicker method that can be done any time of year.
2. **Equipment:** Sun drying does not require any special equipment, while oven drying requires an oven and baking sheets.
3. **Space:** Sun drying requires a lot of space for the drying racks, while oven drying can be done in a small space.
4. **Flavor and texture:** Sun drying produces a unique flavor and texture, while oven drying can result in a consistent quality product but may not have the same unique qualities.

Ultimately, the decision between sun drying and oven drying comes down to personal preference and the resources available. If you have plenty of space and time, and want a unique flavor and texture, sun drying may be the best option. If you want a quicker and more efficient method, oven drying may be the better choice.

CHAPTER 9:
Smoking Fish for Preservation

Smoking is a popular method for preserving fish that has been used for centuries. The process involves exposing the fish to smoke from burning wood or other materials, which imparts a distinct flavor and helps to preserve the fish by dehydrating it and inhibiting the growth of bacteria. In this chapter, we will explore the benefits and techniques of smoking fish for preservation.

Benefits of Smoking Fish

There are several benefits to smoking fish for preservation:
1. **Flavor:** Smoking imparts a unique and delicious flavor to the fish that is highly sought after.
2. **Preservation:** Smoking helps to preserve the fish by dehydrating it and inhibiting the growth of bacteria, making it last longer.
3. **Convenience:** Smoked fish is a convenient and easy-to-store food item that can be used in a variety of dishes.

Techniques for Smoking Fish

There are several techniques for smoking fish, including hot smoking and cold smoking.

Hot Smoking

Hot smoking involves exposing the fish to smoke and heat, usually at a temperature of around 150-180 degrees Fahrenheit. This process cooks the fish and imparts a smoky flavor. Hot smoked fish can be eaten immediately or stored in the refrigerator or freezer for later use.

Cold Smoking

Cold smoking involves exposing the fish to smoke at a lower temperature, usually between 70-90 degrees Fahrenheit. This process does not cook the fish, but rather dries it out and adds a smoky flavor. Cold smoked fish is typically cured with salt and sugar before being smoked, and must be refrigerated or frozen to prevent spoilage.

Equipment for Smoking Fish

The equipment needed for smoking fish includes a smoker, wood chips or sawdust, and a heat source. Smokers can be purchased in a variety of sizes and styles, from small electric models to large outdoor smokers. Different types of wood can be used for smoking, each imparting a unique flavor to the fish. Common woods used for smoking include hickory, apple, cherry, and mesquite.

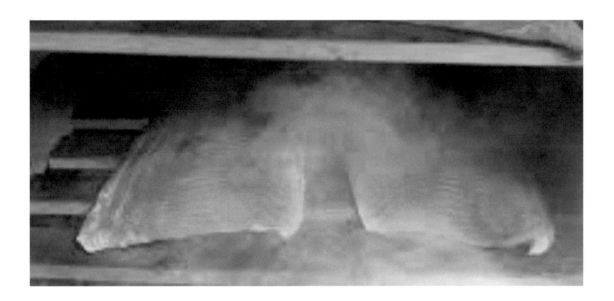

Tips for Smoking Fish

Here are some tips for smoking fish for preservation:
1. Use fresh, high-quality fish that is free of bruises or other damage.
2. Properly prepare the fish by removing the head, tail, and internal organs.
3. Brine the fish before smoking to add flavor and moisture.
4. Use the appropriate temperature and smoking time for the type of fish being smoked.
5. Store smoked fish in airtight containers in the refrigerator or freezer to maintain freshness.

In conclusion, smoking is an effective and delicious method for preserving fish. With the right equipment, technique, and preparation, you can create flavorful and long-lasting smoked fish for use in a variety of dishes.

CHAPTER 10:
Seasoning and Flavoring Dried Fish

Drying fish is an effective method for preserving it, but it can also result in a bland and unappetizing final product. To enhance the flavor of dried fish, various seasonings and flavorings can be added during the drying process or before consumption. In this chapter, we will explore the different ways to season and flavor dried fish.

Seasonings and Flavorings for Dried Fish

There are several seasonings and flavorings that can be used to enhance the taste of dried fish, including:

1. **Salt:** Salt is a common seasoning used to enhance the natural flavor of fish. It can be added during the drying process or sprinkled on the fish before consumption.

2. **Sugar:** Sugar can be used to balance the saltiness of the fish and add a touch of sweetness. It can be added to the brine solution used to cure the fish or sprinkled on the fish before drying.

3. **Spices:** Various spices such as black pepper, cayenne pepper, paprika, garlic powder, and onion powder can be used to add flavor to dried fish. These can be sprinkled on the fish before drying or added to the brine solution.

4. **Herbs:** Fresh or dried herbs such as thyme, rosemary, and parsley can be added to the brine solution or sprinkled on the fish before drying.

5. **Marinades:** Marinades can be used to add flavor to the fish before or after drying. A simple marinade can be made by combining olive oil, lemon juice, garlic, and herbs.

Techniques for Seasoning and Flavoring Dried Fish

There are several techniques for seasoning and flavoring dried fish, including:
1. Adding seasonings to the brine solution used to cure the fish.
2. Sprinkling seasonings on the fish before drying.
3. Using a marinade to add flavor to the fish before or after drying.
4. Mixing the dried fish with other ingredients to create a flavorful dish, such as adding it to soups, stews, or salads.

Tips for Seasoning and Flavoring Dried Fish

Here are some tips for seasoning and flavoring dried fish:
1. Use high-quality seasonings and flavorings to ensure the best taste.
2. Experiment with different combinations of seasonings to find the perfect flavor for your tastes.
3. Use only a small amount of seasoning at a time, as dried fish can easily become over-seasoned.
4. Consider the type of fish being used and choose seasonings that complement its natural flavor.
5. Store seasoned and flavored dried fish in airtight containers to maintain freshness.

In conclusion, seasoning and flavoring dried fish can help to enhance its taste and make it more appetizing. With a variety of seasonings and flavorings to choose from and various techniques to apply them, it's easy to create a delicious and flavorful dried fish.

CHAPTER 11:
Storing and Packaging Dried Fish

After the fish has been dried and seasoned to perfection, it's important to store and package it properly to ensure its longevity and maintain its quality. In this chapter, we will explore the best ways to store and package dried fish.

Storing Dried Fish

Proper storage is crucial for maintaining the quality and safety of dried fish. Here are some tips for storing dried fish:

1. **Keep it in a cool, dry place:** Store dried fish in a cool, dry place away from direct sunlight and humidity. Excessive heat and moisture can cause the fish to spoil and become moldy.
2. **Use airtight containers:** Store dried fish in airtight containers to prevent moisture and air from entering. This will help to maintain its freshness and flavor.
3. **Label the container:** Label the container with the date of drying and the type of fish. This will help you keep track of the shelf life and ensure that you are consuming the oldest fish first.
4. **Store in the refrigerator or freezer:** If you plan to keep the dried fish for an extended period, it's best to store it in the refrigerator or freezer. This will help to prevent spoilage and maintain its quality.

Packaging Dried Fish

Proper packaging is essential for preserving the quality and safety of dried fish during storage and transportation. Here are some tips for packaging dried fish:

1. **Use food-grade packaging:** Use food-grade packaging materials such as plastic bags, vacuum-sealed bags, or aluminum foil. Avoid using materials that may contain harmful chemicals.
2. **Remove air from the packaging:** If using plastic bags or vacuum-sealed bags, make sure to remove as much air as possible. This will help to prevent oxidation and maintain the freshness of the fish.
3. **Label the packaging:** Label the packaging with the type of fish, date of drying, and any other relevant information. This will help you keep track of the fish and ensure that you are consuming the oldest fish first.
4. **Store in a cool, dry place:** Store the packaged dried fish in a cool, dry place away from direct sunlight and humidity.

In conclusion, proper storage and packaging are crucial for maintaining the quality and safety of dried fish. By following the tips outlined in this chapter, you can ensure that your dried fish remains fresh and flavorful for an extended period.

CHAPTER 12:
Hygiene and Safety Considerations

When it comes to handling and processing dried fish, hygiene and safety are of utmost importance. In this chapter, we will discuss some essential hygiene and safety considerations to keep in mind when handling dried fish.

1.   Cleanliness

Maintaining a clean environment is crucial when handling dried fish. Make sure that your processing area is clean and free from any potential contaminants. Wash your hands thoroughly before handling dried fish, and make sure that all utensils and equipment are cleaned and sanitized before use.

2.   Proper Handling

Dried fish can be a potential source of foodborne illness if not handled properly. Always handle dried fish with care and avoid cross-contamination. Keep dried fish away from raw foods and use separate utensils and cutting boards to avoid cross-contamination.

3.   Storage

Proper storage is essential for maintaining the quality and safety of dried fish. Make sure that the storage area is clean, dry, and free from pests. Store dried fish in airtight containers to prevent contamination, and label the containers with the date of drying and type of fish.

4.   Temperature Control

Temperature control is crucial for preventing spoilage and bacterial growth. Keep dried fish at a cool temperature, away from direct sunlight and humidity. If storing for an extended period, consider storing in a refrigerator or freezer.

5.   Personal Protective Equipment

When handling dried fish, it's important to use personal protective equipment such as gloves and masks. This will help to prevent the spread of bacteria and contamination.

6.   Quality Control

Regular quality control checks should be performed to ensure that the dried fish is safe for consumption. Check for signs of spoilage, such as a rancid smell, mold, or discoloration.

In conclusion, hygiene and safety considerations are crucial when handling and processing dried fish. By following the tips outlined in this chapter, you can ensure that your dried fish is safe for consumption and of the highest quality.

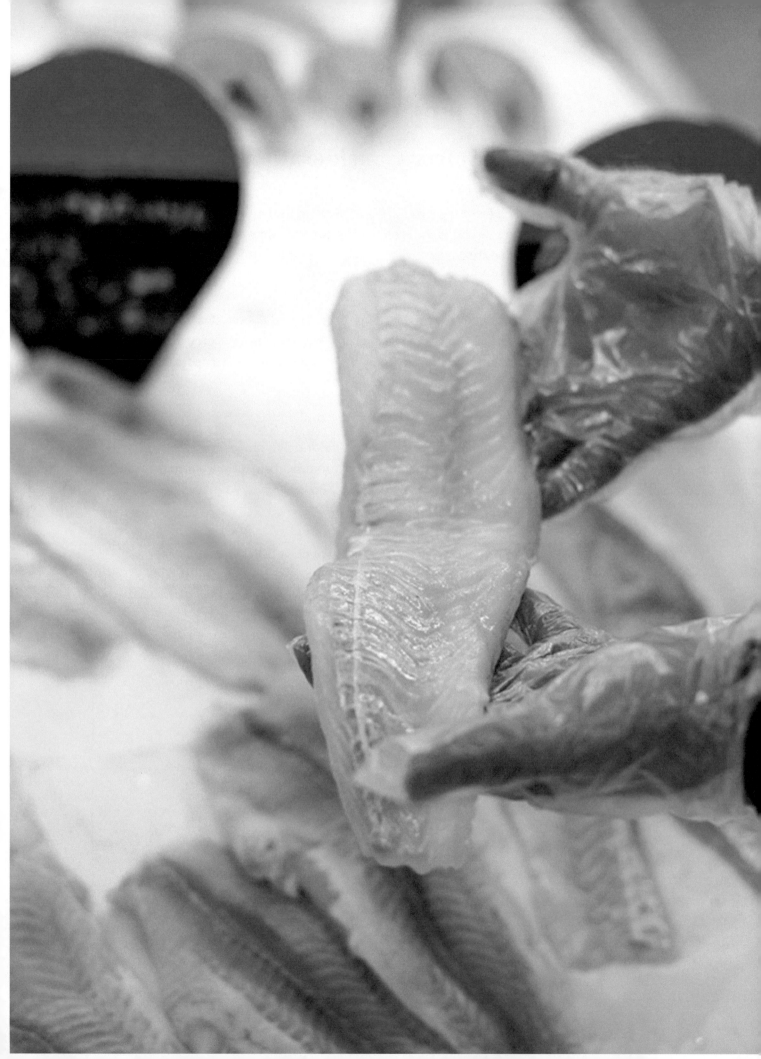

CHAPTER 13:
Selling and Marketing Dried Fish

Dried fish is a popular food item in many cultures around the world, and there is a growing demand for high-quality dried fish products. In this chapter, we will discuss some tips for selling and marketing dried fish.

1.   Know your Target Market
Before selling dried fish, it's important to understand your target market. Consider factors such as age, ethnicity, and dietary preferences when developing your marketing strategy.

2.   Packaging
Packaging is an essential aspect of selling dried fish. The packaging should be attractive and informative, including information about the type of fish, the drying method used, and the date of drying.

3.   Branding
Developing a strong brand is essential for standing out in a competitive market. Consider developing a unique logo and tagline that will help to distinguish your dried fish products from others.

4.   Pricing
Pricing is a critical factor in the success of any business. Consider factors such as the cost of production, competition, and the value of your product when setting your prices.

5.   Distribution
Consider different distribution channels, such as online marketplaces, local markets, and grocery stores, when selling dried fish. Develop relationships with distributors and retailers to help get your products in front of potential customers.

6.   Sampling
Offering samples is a great way to introduce potential customers to your dried fish products. Consider offering samples at local markets or events to help raise awareness of your brand and products.

7.   Promotion
Consider different marketing channels, such as social media, advertising, and public relations, when promoting your dried fish products. Develop a marketing plan that targets your ideal customers and includes promotions and discounts to encourage sales.

In conclusion, selling and marketing dried fish can be a profitable business opportunity. By understanding your target market, developing a strong brand, and utilizing effective marketing strategies, you can successfully sell and market your dried fish products.

CHAPTER 14:
Cooking with Dried Fish

Dried fish is a versatile ingredient that can be used in a variety of recipes. It adds a unique flavor and texture to dishes, making it a popular ingredient in many cultures around the world. In this chapter, we will discuss some tips for cooking with dried fish.

1.   Rehydrating

Before cooking with dried fish, it's important to rehydrate it. Soak the dried fish in cold water for at least 30 minutes, or until it has softened. Drain the water and rinse the fish before using it in your recipe.

2.   Flavor Pairings

Dried fish has a distinctive flavor that pairs well with a variety of ingredients. Some popular flavor pairings include coconut milk, chili peppers, tomatoes, and onions. Experiment with different flavors to find the perfect combination for your recipe.

3.   Texture

Dried fish can add a unique texture to dishes, from crispy to chewy. Consider the texture of the dried fish when deciding how to use it in your recipe. For example, crispy dried fish can be used as a topping for salads or soups, while softer dried fish can be used in stews or curries.

4.   Recipe Ideas

There are many different ways to incorporate dried fish into your cooking. Here are some recipe ideas to get you started:

- **Fried Rice with Dried Fish:** Sauté cooked rice with onions, garlic, and diced dried fish for a flavorful and filling meal.
- **Fish Cakes:** Mix rehydrated dried fish with mashed potatoes and seasonings to make delicious fish cakes.
- **Dried Fish Curry:** Cook dried fish with coconut milk, curry paste, and vegetables for a spicy and satisfying curry dish.
- **Spicy Dried Fish Soup:** Add rehydrated dried fish to a spicy tomato-based soup for a flavorful and hearty meal.

5.   Storage

If you have leftover dried fish after cooking, store it in an airtight container in a cool, dry place. It will keep for several months, making it a convenient ingredient to have on hand for future recipes.

In conclusion, dried fish is a versatile ingredient that can add unique flavor and texture to a variety of recipes. By rehydrating the fish, experimenting with different flavors, and using it in a variety of dishes, you can take advantage of the many benefits of cooking with dried fish.

Drying fish has been a method of preserving seafood for centuries and has played a significant role in the culture and traditions of many coastal communities around the world. The cultural significance of drying fish can be seen in various aspects, including food, economy, and social practices.

Food

Dried fish has been a staple food in many cultures, particularly in areas where fresh seafood is not readily available or during times of the year when fishing is not possible. In many coastal communities, drying fish is a traditional way of preserving and storing seafood, ensuring that it is available to eat year-round. In some cultures, dried fish is also considered a delicacy and is often served at special occasions and celebrations.

Economy

The production and sale of dried fish have also been an important part of the economy in many coastal communities. Drying fish provides a way for fishermen to preserve their catch, which they can then sell in markets or use as a means of trade. In some communities, the production of dried fish has become a significant industry, providing employment and income for many people.

Social Practices

The process of drying fish has also played a role in social practices and traditions. In some cultures, the act of drying fish is a communal activity that brings people together. Families and neighbors work together to clean and prepare the fish, and then the fish is laid out to dry in the sun. This process provides an opportunity for people to socialize and share stories and traditions.

In addition, the consumption of dried fish is often tied to cultural practices and beliefs. In some cultures, dried fish is used in religious ceremonies or as an offering to ancestors or spirits. The cultural significance of dried fish can also be seen in the various ways it is prepared and served, with each culture having its own unique recipes and methods.

In conclusion, the cultural significance of drying fish is evident in the various ways it has been used and valued in many coastal communities. From providing a reliable source of food to supporting local economies and social practices, drying fish has played a vital role in the traditions and cultures of many people around the world.

THE ART OF DRY-AGING TUNA
Techniques and Recipes for a Unique and Flavorful Experience

Intro:

Dry-aging is a process that has been used for centuries to enhance the flavor and texture of meats like beef and pork. However, many people are unaware that dry-aging can also be applied to seafood, specifically tuna. Dry-aged tuna has a unique and intense flavor that sets it apart from fresh tuna and is highly prized by seafood aficionados.

In this book, we will explore the art of dry-aging tuna, from the traditional Japanese method of aging to modern dry-aging techniques. You will learn about the history and cultural significance of dry-aged tuna and how the process of dry-aging affects the flavor, texture, and overall quality of the fish. We will also provide recipes and cooking tips for making the most of this delicious and flavorful ingredient.

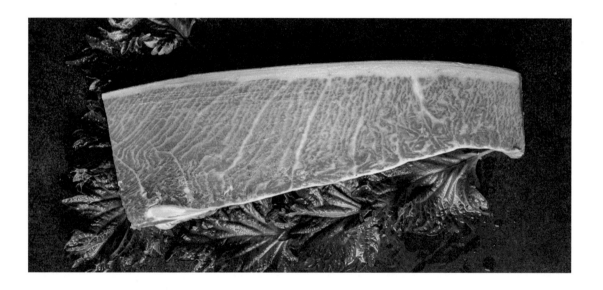

But why dry-age tuna? The answer lies in the complex chemical and biological processes that occur during the aging process. When tuna is dry-aged, it undergoes a transformation that results in a more concentrated flavor and a firmer texture. This is due to the breakdown of enzymes in the fish, which results in the production of umami compounds that give the tuna its distinctive flavor. The drying process also removes excess moisture from the fish, resulting in a denser texture and a more concentrated flavor.

Dry-aged tuna has a rich cultural history, particularly in Japan where it has been a prized ingredient for centuries. The traditional Japanese method of aging tuna, known as katsuo-bushi, involves smoking and drying the fish for several months, resulting in a product that is used as a flavoring agent in many Japanese dishes.

Today, there are a variety of dry-aging techniques used to age tuna, including both traditional and modern methods. In this book, we will explore these techniques and provide guidance on how to select and prepare the best dry-aged tuna for your cooking needs.

Whether you are a seafood lover, a professional chef, or simply looking to expand your culinary horizons, "The Art of Dry-Aging Tuna" will introduce you to a new world of flavor and texture. With detailed information on the science and history of dry-aged tuna, as well as recipes and cooking tips, this book is the ultimate guide to this unique and flavorful ingredient.

CHAPTER 16.1
What is Dry-Aged Tuna?

Dry-aged tuna is a type of tuna that has been aged for a period of time in a controlled environment with low humidity and precise temperature. During the aging process, enzymes in the fish break down the muscle fibers and connective tissue, resulting in a more tender and flavorful product.

Traditionally, dry-aged tuna has been a staple of Japanese cuisine, where it is known as katsuobushi. In Japan, the process of dry-aging tuna is highly revered, and it has been perfected over centuries of practice. The Japanese have developed a specific method for dry-aging tuna that involves hanging the fish in a cool, dry place for several months.

Today, dry-aged tuna is becoming increasingly popular in other parts of the world, and new techniques have been developed to produce similar results in a shorter amount of time. One such technique is called wet aging, where tuna is vacuum-sealed and aged in a refrigerated environment. Another technique is called salt-curing, where tuna is coated in a layer of salt and aged in a controlled environment.

Dry-aged tuna can be sold in a variety of forms, including whole loins, steaks, and flakes. It is often used as a flavor enhancer in dishes such as soups, stews, and sauces, and it can also be eaten on its own as a snack or appetizer.

One example of a dish that features dry-aged tuna is seared tuna with a soy-ginger glaze. The dry-aged tuna adds an intense umami flavor to the dish, which complements the sweet and savory glaze. Another example is tuna tataki, which is made by searing thinly sliced tuna and serving it with a dipping sauce. The dry-aged tuna in this dish provides a unique and complex flavor profile that elevates the dish to new heights.

Overall, dry-aged tuna is a unique and flavorful product that is highly prized in many parts of the world. By understanding what dry-aged tuna is and how it is produced, we can appreciate its unique qualities and explore new ways to use it in our cooking.

CHAPTER 16.2
The Science of Dry-Aging Tuna

In this chapter, we will delve into the science behind dry-aging tuna and how it affects the flavor, texture, and quality of the fish. We will explore the enzymatic and biochemical changes that occur during the aging process and how they impact the final product.

One of the key factors in dry-aging tuna is the breakdown of enzymes in the fish. Proteolytic enzymes are responsible for breaking down the muscle fibers in the fish, which results in a more tender and flavorful product. One example of such an enzyme is cathepsin B, which is known to play a significant role in the dry-aging process of tuna.

In addition to enzymatic changes, dry-aging also leads to biochemical changes in the fish. One such change is the production of umami compounds, which give dry-aged tuna its unique and intense flavor. Umami is a Japanese term that refers to the fifth taste, which is savory and meaty. When tuna is dry-aged, the breakdown of proteins leads to the production of glutamate and other amino acids that contribute to the umami flavor.

To illustrate the importance of these enzymatic and biochemical changes, let's compare the flavor of fresh tuna to dry-aged tuna. Fresh tuna has a mild flavor that is often described as buttery or nutty. However, when tuna is dry-aged, the flavor becomes much more intense and complex, with notes of umami, earthiness, and even a hint of sweetness.

Another important factor in dry-aging tuna is the amount of time the fish is aged. Traditional Japanese methods involve aging tuna for several months, but modern techniques can produce similar results in a matter of days or weeks. The length of time the tuna is aged can have a significant impact on the flavor and texture of the fish, with longer aging times resulting in a more intense flavor and firmer texture.

Overall, this chapter lays the foundation for understanding the science behind dry-aging tuna and how it produces a unique and flavorful product. By exploring the enzymatic and biochemical changes that occur during the aging process, we can gain a deeper appreciation for the art of dry-aging tuna and the delicious results it produces.

CHAPTER 16.3
Traditional Japanese Tuna Aging Methods

As mentioned in the previous chapter, traditional Japanese tuna aging, known as katsuobushi, is a highly revered and time-honored process that has been perfected over centuries. The process involves taking freshly caught tuna, typically of the skipjack variety, and transforming it into a dried, hardened form that can be stored for long periods of time without spoiling.

The first step in the process is to clean and fillet the tuna, removing the head, tail, and internal organs. The resulting loins are then soaked in saltwater to remove any residual blood and impurities. Once the loins have been cleaned, they are hung up to dry in a cool, dry place with low humidity. This allows the loins to gradually lose moisture and firm up.

After several months of drying, the loins are ready to be smoked. Traditionally, the tuna is smoked over a fire made from cherry wood, which imparts a distinctive smoky flavor. The smoking process also helps to further dehydrate the tuna, creating a hardened and long-lasting product.

Once the smoking process is complete, the tuna is left to cool and then shaved into thin flakes using a special tool called a katsuobushi kezuriki. The flakes are then ready to be used in a variety of dishes, including soups, stews, and sauces.

One of the most famous dishes to feature katsuobushi is dashi, a Japanese soup stock that forms the basis of many traditional Japanese dishes. Dashi is made by boiling katsuobushi flakes and kombu, a type of seaweed, in water. The resulting broth is then strained and used as a base for soups, stews, and sauces.

Another popular dish that features katsuobushi is okonomiyaki, a savory pancake made with cabbage, seafood, and a variety of other ingredients. Katsuobushi flakes are often sprinkled on top of the finished dish, adding a smoky, umami flavor.

Overall, traditional Japanese tuna aging methods are a testament to the skill and expertise of Japanese chefs and food producers. By taking the time to carefully dry and smoke the tuna, they are able to create a unique and highly prized product that is revered around the world.

CHAPTER 16.4
The different parts of the tuna that are commonly aged using traditional Japanese methods are:

1. **Otoro -** This is the most sought-after and prized part of the tuna, and is characterized by its high fat content and rich flavor. The belly of the tuna is typically cut into large sections and aged for a period of 6 months to 1 year or even longer, depending on the desired flavor and texture. During this time, the otoro is carefully monitored for temperature and humidity levels to ensure that it is aging properly. As the fat content of the otoro is broken down over time, the texture becomes softer and more buttery, and the flavor becomes more complex and intense.

2. **Chutoro -** The middle section of the tuna belly has a slightly lower fat content compared to otoro, but is still highly prized for its rich flavor and texture. Chutoro is typically aged for a period of 6-12 months, depending on the desired flavor and texture. Like otoro, the temperature and humidity levels of the aging environment are carefully monitored to ensure that the chutoro is aging properly. As the fat content is broken down over time, the texture becomes softer and more buttery, and the flavor becomes more complex and intense.

3. **Akami** - This is the leaner part of the tuna, which is typically used for sashimi and sushi. Akami is aged for a shorter period of time compared to the belly cuts, typically 2-3 months. The aging process for akami is different from that of the belly cuts, as the goal is to achieve a firmer texture rather than a buttery one. The aging environment is still carefully monitored for temperature and humidity levels, but the length of time and the desired texture and flavor profile are different.

In addition to temperature and humidity levels, other factors can also affect the aging process, such as the size of the fish and the aging environment. For example, larger tuna may require longer aging periods to fully develop the desired flavor and texture, while smaller tuna may require less time. The aging environment must also be carefully controlled to prevent spoilage and ensure that the tuna is aging properly.

Overall, the traditional Japanese tuna aging methods are a testament to the skill and expertise of Japanese food producers and chefs. The careful balance of time, temperature, and humidity ensures that the fish is transformed into a dried, hardened form that can be stored for long periods of time without spoiling. The result is a uniquely flavorful and textured tuna that is highly prized by sushi and sashimi aficionados around the world.

CHAPTER 16.5
Modern Dry-Aging Techniques

In addition to the traditional Japanese tuna aging methods, modern dry-aging techniques have been developed to meet the demand for high-quality aged tuna in the global market. These methods incorporate technological advancements and scientific knowledge to improve the consistency and efficiency of the aging process.

One modern dry-aging technique involves using special aging chambers or cabinets that control the temperature, humidity, and airflow around the tuna. These chambers are designed to mimic the natural aging environment of the fish, but with greater precision and control. For example, some aging chambers use ultraviolet light to simulate the effects of sunlight on the aging process, while others use specialized fans to circulate the air and prevent mold growth. Another modern technique involves vacuum-sealing the tuna to remove excess moisture and speed up the aging process. The vacuum-sealed tuna is then placed in a controlled environment to age for a set period of time. This method is especially useful for smaller cuts of tuna, as it can reduce the aging time needed to achieve the desired texture and flavor.

One advantage of modern dry-aging techniques is the ability to age tuna year-round, regardless of season or climate. Traditional tuna aging methods rely on natural fluctuations in temperature and humidity, which can be difficult to replicate in different regions or seasons. Modern aging techniques, however, allow for consistent and controlled aging conditions regardless of external factors.

Another advantage is the ability to experiment with different aging times and techniques to achieve specific flavor and texture profiles. With precise control over temperature, humidity, and other variables, chefs and food producers can create unique and customized aged tuna products.

Despite the benefits of modern dry-aging techniques, some purists argue that they lack the authenticity and nuance of traditional methods. They also point out that the use of technology and artificial environments may compromise the natural flavor and texture of the tuna. However, many modern dry-aged tuna products have received high praise from chefs and consumers alike, demonstrating the potential for innovation and improvement in the world of tuna aging.

Overall, modern dry-aging techniques offer an alternative approach to traditional Japanese tuna aging methods, with advantages in consistency, efficiency, and customization. While some may argue that they lack the authenticity of traditional methods, the results speak for themselves, with high-quality aged tuna products available year-round to meet the demand of sushi and sashimi enthusiasts around the world.

Selecting and preparing dry-aged tuna is a critical step in achieving the best flavor and texture from this delicacy. Here are some tips on how to choose the right dry-aged tuna and prepare it for serving.

CHAPTER 16.6
Selecting and Preparing Dry-Aged Tuna

Selecting Dry-Aged Tuna When selecting dry-aged tuna, consider the following factors:

1. **Color:** The tuna should have a deep red or pink color, with no brown or gray spots.
2. **Texture:** The flesh should be firm, but not too tough or dry. It should be easy to slice with a sharp knife.
3. **Smell:** The tuna should have a fresh, clean smell with a slight ocean scent. Avoid tuna with a strong fishy odor.
4. **Source:** Choose tuna from a reputable supplier that uses sustainable and responsible fishing practices.

Preparing Dry-Aged Tuna Once you have selected your dry-aged tuna, it's time to prepare it for serving. Here are some steps to follow:

1. **Thawing:** If your tuna is frozen, it should be thawed slowly in the refrigerator for several hours before serving. Do not thaw tuna at room temperature or in warm water, as this can cause the fish to spoil.
2. **Cleaning:** Remove any skin or bones from the tuna before slicing. Rinse the tuna under cold water to remove any scales or debris.
3. **Slicing:** Use a sharp, non-serrated knife to slice the tuna against the grain into thin, even pieces. For sashimi, aim for slices that are about 1/4 inch thick. For sushi, slices should be slightly thinner.
4. **Serving:** Dry-aged tuna is best served raw, either as sashimi or sushi. Arrange the slices on a platter or individual plates, and serve with wasabi, soy sauce, and pickled ginger.

Storage of Dry-Aged Tuna Dry-aged tuna should be stored in the refrigerator at a temperature between 32-39°F. It should be consumed within 24 hours of preparation, as it can spoil quickly. Avoid storing dry-aged tuna in the freezer, as this can compromise the texture and flavor of the fish.

By following these tips, you can ensure that you are selecting and preparing the best dry-aged tuna for your sushi and sashimi dishes. Remember to choose high-quality tuna from a reputable supplier, and handle it with care to preserve its delicate flavor and texture.

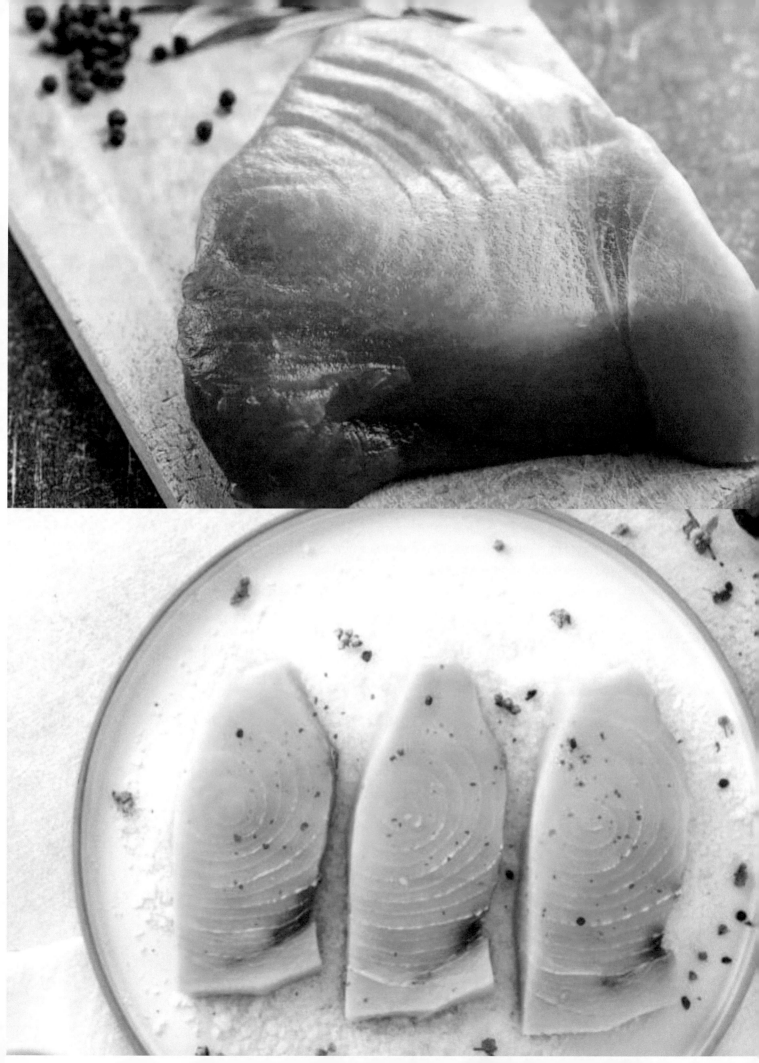

CHAPTER 16.7
Cooking with Dry-Aged Tuna

Cooking with dry-aged tuna is a wonderful way to enjoy its rich, complex flavors and textures. In this chapter, we will explore the different ways that dry-aged tuna can be used in Japanese and modern cuisine.

Japanese Cuisine In Japanese cuisine, dry-aged tuna is often used in sashimi and sushi dishes. The rich, buttery flavor of the tuna pairs well with the simple, clean flavors of Japanese cuisine. Here are some traditional Japanese dishes that use dry-aged tuna:

1. **Maguro no Kama Yaki:** This is a popular Japanese dish that is made by grilling the collar of the tuna, which is a fatty and flavorful cut. The tuna collar is seasoned with soy sauce, sake, and mirin, and then grilled until it is crispy on the outside and tender on the inside.

2. **Maguro no Tataki:** This dish involves lightly searing the surface of the tuna, then thinly slicing it and serving it with grated ginger, garlic, and soy sauce.

3. **Maguro Donburi:** This is a rice bowl dish that consists of a bed of rice topped with thinly sliced tuna, avocado, and other toppings such as cucumber, seaweed, and sesame seeds.

Modern Cuisine Dry-aged tuna is also used in modern cuisine, where chefs experiment with new techniques and flavors. Here are some examples of how dry-aged tuna is used in modern cuisine:

1. **Dry-aged tuna tartare:** This dish involves finely chopping the dry-aged tuna and mixing it with ingredients like capers, shallots, and herbs to create a flavorful and elegant appetizer.

2. **Dry-aged tuna carpaccio:** Thin slices of dry-aged tuna are arranged on a plate and served with a drizzle of olive oil, lemon juice, and salt, creating a simple and delicious dish.

3. **Dry-aged tuna burgers:** Dry-aged tuna can be used to make burgers that are healthier than traditional beef burgers. The tuna is ground up and mixed with herbs, spices, and breadcrumbs to create a flavorful and nutritious patty.

In all of these dishes, the key to using dry-aged tuna is to let the natural flavors of the fish shine through. Whether you are preparing a traditional Japanese dish or a modern creation, the rich, buttery flavor of dry-aged tuna is sure to delight your taste buds.

CHAPTER 16.8
Pairing Wine with Dry-Aged Tuna

Pairing Wine with Dry-Aged Tuna

Dry-aged tuna is a delicacy that is often enjoyed with a fine glass of wine. The complex flavors and textures of the tuna make it a versatile ingredient that pairs well with a variety of wines. In this chapter, we will explore the best wine pairings for dry-aged tuna.

White Wines

White wines are a great choice for pairing with dry-aged tuna. The light, refreshing flavors of white wine complement the rich, buttery flavor of the tuna without overpowering it. Some popular white wines to pair with dry-aged tuna include:

1. **Sauvignon Blanc:** The crisp, citrusy flavors of Sauvignon Blanc pair well with the delicate flavor of dry-aged tuna.
2. **Chardonnay:** The rich, buttery flavors of Chardonnay complement the buttery texture of the tuna.
3. **Pinot Grigio:** The light, refreshing flavors of Pinot Grigio are a perfect match for the delicate flavor of dry-aged tuna.

Red Wines

While red wine is not typically paired with fish, dry-aged tuna can be an exception due to its meaty and complex flavors. Here are some red wines that pair well with dry-aged tuna:

1. **Pinot Noir:** The light, fruity flavors of Pinot Noir complement the delicate flavor of dry-aged tuna without overpowering it.
2. **Syrah:** The rich, bold flavors of Syrah pair well with the meaty texture of the tuna.

3. Merlot: The soft, fruity flavors of Merlot complement the delicate flavor of dry-aged tuna.

Rose Wines

Rose wines are another great option for pairing with dry-aged tuna. The light, refreshing flavors of rose wines complement the delicate flavor of the tuna without overpowering it. Some popular rose wines to pair with dry-aged tuna include:

1. Provencal Rose: The light, floral flavors of Provencal Rose are a great match for the delicate flavor of dry-aged tuna.
2. White Zinfandel: The fruity flavors of White Zinfandel complement the meaty texture of the tuna.
3. Sparkling Rose: The light, refreshing bubbles of Sparkling Rose pair well with the delicate flavor of dry-aged tuna.

In conclusion, dry-aged tuna is a versatile ingredient that pairs well with a variety of wines. Whether you prefer white, red, or rose wine, there is a perfect pairing for your dry-aged tuna dish. By experimenting with different wines, you can find the perfect match to bring out the best flavors in your dry-aged tuna.

CHAPTER 16.9:
The Future of Dry-Aged Tuna

Dry-aged tuna has been a delicacy in Japan for centuries, but it has only recently gained popularity in Western cuisine. As more people discover the unique and complex flavors of dry-aged tuna, the demand for this delicacy is likely to increase. However, as the demand for dry-aged tuna grows, there are concerns about the sustainability of the tuna population and the environmental impact of the aging process.

Sustainable Tuna Fishing

The traditional method of catching tuna involves using large nets that can scoop up entire schools of fish, including non-target species like dolphins and sea turtles. This method, known as purse seine fishing, can be devastating to marine ecosystems. To ensure the future of dry-aged tuna, it is important to promote sustainable tuna fishing practices that minimize bycatch and protect the marine environment.

One such method is pole-and-line fishing, where fishermen use a single hook and line to catch one tuna at a time. This method reduces the amount of bycatch and allows fishermen to target only mature tuna, which helps to maintain healthy tuna populations. Another method is to use FADs (Fish Aggregating Devices), which are floating devices that attract tuna, allowing fishermen to catch them without the need for large nets.

Alternative Aging Methods

Traditional Japanese dry-aging methods involve aging the tuna in a special environment, with strict temperature and humidity control. However, this process can be time-consuming and expensive, making it difficult to produce dry-aged tuna in large quantities. To meet the growing demand for dry-aged tuna, some producers are exploring alternative aging methods that are faster and more cost-effective.

One such method is called "wet aging," where the tuna is aged in a vacuum-sealed bag with its own juices. This method can produce similar flavor and texture to traditional dry-aging, but in a fraction of the time. Another method is to use special enzymes to break down the proteins in the tuna, creating a similar texture to dry-aging without the need for a special aging environment.

Innovation in Cuisine

As more chefs and home cooks experiment with dry-aged tuna, there is a growing trend towards using this ingredient in new and innovative ways. Some chefs are using dry-aged tuna in traditional Japanese dishes like sushi and sashimi, while others are using it in modern fusion dishes like tuna tartare or dry-aged tuna tacos.

There is also growing interest in using dry-aged tuna as a sustainable alternative to other types of meat. The meaty texture of dry-aged tuna makes it a great substitute for beef or pork in dishes like burgers or meatballs. As more people look for sustainable and healthy protein sources, dry-aged tuna could become a popular ingredient in a variety of cuisines.

In conclusion, the future of dry-aged tuna is bright, with growing interest in this delicacy around the world. To ensure the sustainability of tuna populations and minimize the environmental impact of aging, it is important to promote sustainable fishing practices and explore alternative aging methods. As chefs and home cooks continue to experiment with this versatile ingredient, we can expect to see new and innovative uses for dry-aged tuna in the years to come.

CHAPTER 16.10:
The Business of Dry-Aged Tuna

Dry-aged tuna is a relatively new concept in the seafood industry, and it has quickly gained popularity among seafood enthusiasts, chefs, and restaurateurs. In this chapter, we will explore the business side of dry-aged tuna and the opportunities it presents.

Supply and Demand

Dry-aged tuna is a premium product that commands a higher price point compared to fresh or frozen tuna. The supply of dry-aged tuna is limited due to the lengthy and careful aging process, which means that the demand for this product is high. This has created an opportunity for seafood suppliers and wholesalers to add dry-aged tuna to their product offerings.
Marketing and Branding

The success of any product in the market depends on its marketing and branding. Dry-aged tuna has a unique selling proposition and a story that can be used to market and promote it. Suppliers and wholesalers can use this story to create a brand around their dry-aged tuna product and differentiate themselves from competitors. This includes highlighting the traditional Japanese aging methods used, the high-quality of the tuna used, and the expertise involved in the aging process.

Restaurant Sales

Restaurants are the primary market for dry-aged tuna, as they are always looking for unique and high-quality products to feature on their menus. Chefs can use dry-aged tuna in a variety of dishes, from sushi to sashimi to ceviche. The unique texture and umami flavor of dry-aged tuna can elevate any dish and create a memorable dining experience for customers.

Consumer Sales

The demand for high-quality seafood has been growing among consumers, and dry-aged tuna is no exception. Consumers are willing to pay a premium for products that are unique and of high-quality, making dry-aged tuna a potential product for direct-to-consumer sales. Seafood suppliers can sell dry-aged tuna to consumers through their websites, social media platforms, or online marketplaces.

Challenges

The business of dry-aged tuna also presents some challenges. The lengthy and careful aging process can result in a high cost of production and a limited supply of the product. Additionally, the high price point of dry-aged tuna can be a barrier for some customers, which can limit its market potential.

CONCLUSION

The business of dry-aged tuna is still in its infancy, but it presents a significant opportunity for seafood suppliers, wholesalers, and restaurateurs. The unique flavor and texture of dry-aged tuna, combined with its traditional Japanese aging methods, make it a premium product that commands a high price point. By understanding the supply and demand dynamics of the market and investing in marketing and branding efforts, businesses can capitalize on the growing demand for this product and create a successful venture in the seafood industry.

Made in the USA
Columbia, SC
20 September 2024

42710077R00038